For Want of Water

The National Poetry Series

The National Poetry Series was founded in 1978 to ensure
the publication of five poetry books annually through five
participating publishers. Publication is funded annually
by the Lannan Foundation, Amazon Literary Partnership,
Barnes & Noble, the Poetry Foundation, the PG Family
Foundation and the Betsy Community Fund, Joan Bingham,
Mariana Cook, Stephen Graham, Juliet Lea Hillman Simonds,
William Kistler, Jeffrey Ravetch, Laura Baudo Sillerman,
and Margaret Thornton. For a complete listing of the
generous contributors to the National Poetry Series,
please visit www.nationalpoetryseries.org.

2016 COMPETITION WINNERS

I Know Your Kind
William Brewer of Brooklyn, New York
Chosen by Ada Limón for Milkweed

For Want of Water
Sasha Pimentel of El Paso, Texas
Chosen by Gregory Pardlo for Beacon Press

Civil Twilight
Jeffrey Schultz of Los Angeles, California
Chosen by David St. John for Ecco

MADNESS
Sam Sax of Austin, Texas
Chosen by Terrance Hayes for Penguin Books

Thaw
Chelsea Dingman of Tampa, Florida
Chosen by Allison Joseph for University of Georgia Press

FOR WANT OF WATER

and other poems

Sasha Pimentel

Beacon Press, Boston

Beacon Press
Boston, Massachusetts
www.beacon.org

Beacon Press books
are published under the auspices of
the Unitarian Universalist Association of Congregations.

Foreword © 2017 by Gregory Pardlo

20 19 18 17   8 7 6 5 4 3 2 1

This book is printed on acid-free paper that meets the uncoated
paper ANSI / NISO specifications for permanence as revised in 1992.

Text design by Nancy Koerner
at Wilsted & Taylor Publishing Services

Library of Congress Cataloging-in-Publication Data

Names: Pimentel, Sasha, author.
Title: For want of water, and other poems / Sasha Pimentel.
Description: Boston : Beacon Press, 2017. | Series: The national poetry series
Identifiers: LCCN 2016052722 (print) | LCCN 2017009684 (ebook) | ISBN 9780807027851
  (paperback) | ISBN 9780807027868 (e-book)
Subjects: | BISAC: POETRY / American / General. | POETRY / American / Asian
  American.
Classification: LCC PS3616.I485 A6 2017 (print) | LCC PS3616.I485 (ebook) |
  DDC 811/.6 — dc23
LC record available at https://lccn.loc.gov/2016052722

for Michael

[*Photo caption / no image*]: While flying over the border between Mexico and the United States, an astronaut aboard the International Space Station photographed these sister cities on the Rio Grande. The image shows the second largest metropolitan area (population 2.7 million people) on the Mexico–US border. The centers of El Paso and Ciudad Juárez (image top right) lie close together on opposite sides of the Rio Grande, and large residential areas cover the arid slopes in the rest of the scene.

. . . kingpins with names like the Engineer, head-chopping hit men, dirty cops and double-dealing politicians. And, of course, there are users—millions of them. Over the past five years, nearly 48,000 people have been killed in suspected drug-related violence in [Juárez] Mexico. . . . In the first three quarters of 2011, almost 13,000 people died. . . . The death toll doesn't include the more than 5,000 people who have disappeared. . . .

[*El Paso, Texas—:*]

CONTENTS

V

FOREWORD

"These are not words of asking," writes Sasha Pimentel in the poem "Orison." Rather, this is "a divining / of intersections"—an apt description of her virtuosic second poetry collection, *For Want of Water*. More concretely, *For Want of Water* is a divining of seams, edges, joints, webs, wings, hinges, and more, an apparently inexhaustible archive of parts that flex and clench in expressions of desire as often as in response to threat. The fusion of elements, distances, the organic, and the inorganic reflects Pimentel's mastery of form. We seem to be everywhere at once in these poems. Her control of imagery and sound creates worlds that are deeply subjective without appearing hallucinatory. A description as surreal as "sweat bubbles / above his lip like caviar" is counterbalanced with images of unadorned precision, like, for example, a drug addict's "thumb, calloused / from the sparkwheel" of a lighter. In this way, Pimentel bridges consciousness and dream.

Borders abound here as well. We can think of a border as a ritual space over which a person's status and relationship to community might change dramatically. Some borders are so powerful that they radiate a culture of violence just to enforce the illusion that the border is real. A border with the power of life and death, like the one between the United States and Mexico, might insist that those who survive crossing it are less human on one side than on the other. How does a poet respond to a landscape burdened with such brutal imagination? Pimentel, a Filipina poet raised in the United States and Saudi Arabia, lives with her family on a farm near the border of Ciudad Juárez, México, in El Paso, Texas. While prepositional phrases in a sentence like the one before this might link neatly and sequentially on the page (*on a farm, in El Paso, with her family*), in reality, the conditions overlap and nest inside one another boundlessly, like sight lines in an M. C. Escher drawing. The personal is political, and the local is global—these aphorisms hold objective weight in Pimentel's poems without surrendering responsibility for perspective and interpretation. These complexities suggest something of Pimentel's relationship to borders and boundaries.

Pimentel often sees borders as expressions of patriarchy projected onto our bodies as well as onto the lands we inhabit. In one poem, an uncle's hand that "split the continent / of this woman's skin, her back reaching out / to him in engorged and broken love" is the same hand that receives "your father's land, compressed / to papers, sealed in plastic, because this is how / we declare what is ours and what isn't." "What is ours" depends on our ability to distinguish it from "what isn't," and this, too, requires a border. It is a testimony to the breadth of her skill that Pimentel can extract personal meaning and truth from this miscellany of perspectives and subject positions.

Pimentel's lyrical style is reminiscent of Larry Levis's in that there are many surprising leaps and discursive digressions that work like cogs urging us forward through the poems. But, calm with the wisdom of endurance, the patron saint of this collection has to be the poet Ai, whose southwestern landscape is echoed here along with its cruel and radiant vitality. Whether the speakers in Pimentel's poems are victims or perpetrators of mortal sins or misdemeanors, the world is rendered with such objectivity that justice is an afterthought, if it comes to mind at all. These poems don't ask for recompense, and the result is a lack of affect more harrowing in its frankness than any attempt to play the reader's heartstrings.

And like Ai, Pimentel has great facility with her dramatis personae and chooses their masks not simply for theatrical value but to explore the multiple tensions inherent in the adaptation. Pimentel flips the argument in Shakespeare's Sonnet 116 to suggest that love indeed admits impediments as time crosscuts the superficial allure of youth and introduces the nostalgia that can challenge a relationship long settled into routines of domesticity. In one sentence, the poem reflects on "The failure of my body to compete with self / as artifact." What is perhaps most striking is how the emotion is heightened in the absence of an active verb. While we don't get stasis or helplessness, the observation is nonetheless poignant. In another poem, Pimentel gives voice to the woman in Gustav Klimt's painting The Kiss. Her choice of perspective alone calls attention to the critical tendency to identify with the male figure in the painting. That the female figure is the unwilling object of this kiss allows for a strikingly novel interpretation.

Consistent with her interest in intersections, Pimentel combines ekphrasis and the dramatic monologue to present an architecture of critique that never once distracts us from its lyric virtuosity. Every poem, similarly, is a three-dimensional chess game of intersecting psychological nuances, lyric figuration, innovative storytelling, and rhetorical devices. Rather than avoiding the politics of gender, nationality, class, and race, Pimentel demonstrates, with a sure hand, that "the personal is political" is no mere bromide but an inspired approach to the very foundations of literary craft.

Gregory Pardlo

I

If I Die in Juárez

The violins in our home are emptied
of sound, strings stilled, missing
fingers. This one can bring a woman down
to her knees, just to hear again
its voice, thick as a callus
from the wooden belly. This one's strings
are broken. And another, open,
is a mouth. I want to kiss
them as I hurt to be kissed, ruin
their brittle necks in the husk of my palm,
my fingers across the bridge, pressing
chord into chord, that delicate protest—:
my tongue rowing the frets, and our throats high
from the silences of keeping.

13 Ways of Knowing Her

I.

Mother tells me a bird is trying to kill her. I tighten. Memory her ticking
eye, opening and closing. Snap on a dress, shell of her breath swallowing the
phone. (Pitch.) The bird sings, kills her softly, minutely.

Now my mother is trilling loudly, high with starling's call.

2.

Only at night do I know her solitude, halo of infomercials, her cramping
cool and yellow leg, and somewhere outside, her husband, the unstruck bell
of morning birds.

3.

I try to ask her where she is.

*Your father took the car when I had an accident; I never drove again. The only place
I can't hear it is the downstairs bathroom; I've been here for a week.* House of her
body, animal in grief. I carry my mother on my shoulder, cage her voice
against my cheek, walk her near-confessions through my home—*una stanza
all'altra*—her single room closing in. Outside my window: Juárez burns.
Her ticking eye must be fluttering already, eye's lid of feathers bobbing to
shadow, *and it's killing me: I can't sleep: and when I wake, it's at the window.* Her
tiles creased with bleach.

I hide my love for birds, and streets.

4.

Nest of my mother's hands:

    shifting and slipping to signs, to an unstruck slap, and once, the vortex
    of a hundred beetles.

5.

I wake to sense a brushing on my neck.

6.

Middle nights she braced her stomach around my knees, whispering, *shh, it's me, it's Mama,* so I wouldn't kick—knew to name her weight so I'd understand it wasn't my father's growing shape. Falling

    wakes: shift

    from the cool center of water, rippling, to the point at which ice

cracks. He came home from work unbuckled, snaked his belt to chill the air, his teeth opaque. Mother helped him hold her children onto the bed.

After, she entered

    our room, clicking like starling, her hands viscous with Vicks, our welts rising, eyelashes glazing cotton. Moonlight hummed, her throat

    vibrating. The medical smell of my mother's wrists.

7.

Susan Wood asks *if grief were a bird,* and my microwave dings.

    Seven men fall to their knees, past the wall, across the border.

    My mouth clot with iron.

Starlings are aggressive; they have been seen evicting bluebirds, kibitzing with blackbirds, are fierce protectors of their young. Shakespeare's Hotspur imagined this creature mimicking *Mortimer, Mortimer!*, beak whistling a man's name *to keep his anger still in motion,* so anglophile near-ornithologists unfold 100 starlings across the ocean into Central Park—into the late 19th century, the sky splattered with calling and leaving.

Father comes too late at the doorknob, my mother's ear hinging to hear his direction.

8.

I buy her a plastic owl on amazon.com.

It's solar-powered, neck pivots, eyes glow.

The adult in me no longer wants to love. Like this. But I remember the prayer of her armpit on my shoulder, her breasts crescent on my nascent own, the smell of carpet and carrying her cramped and dragging legs. *Mortimer!*—, my mother—

her voice on the phone sobbing my name keeps my anger still in motion, and I click for priority ship.

9.

I come home from work and my husband's crying. The sky louvered with smoke. He holds one of our chickens, cave of her throat slipped from the dog's mouth. Her eye. Glossy as moon.

Her feathers rise and fall.

El Diario: Marcan siete asesinatos el fin de semana, and

I curl my palm around her neck.

10.

The next day her voice is high. She's stroking the carved plastic crown from the box.

Gifted. Gratitude. (We're all so grateful to be alive.)

I tell her to spear the fake owl next to the weeping willow, let its head quiver with each rotation. I clink ice inside my glass, cradle my mother hot room to room.

II.

Tile edges her sobbing.

She wants to know where my father is.

(Accordion: my knuckles.) I remember the floor, fibers floating the hallway, the uneven pitch of her whines, my father's crackling breath.

But the bird continues to sing. *I'm sorry*, I say, *I'm sorry*.

Memories of waking:

> Clouds creamy with snow.
>
> Startling black flight from the magnolia—
>
> Talcum powder winged from my mother's hands. And the sound of a piano hinge, the unplayed key.

Before my mother hobbles, she counts, necessary ritual to leave a room: each light switch whipping on and off, 13 times. She's resigned herself from stairs. Grief, and in Arkansas, a dead dark sea of birds.

12.

We mark the edge of one of many circles. I try to tell my husband about my mother's starling. He grips my hand, clamps in my sweat. I no longer want to listen. We're on the backyard swing. We rock to the dying light. From an open window a phone rings, crying its bird-like cymbals. My mother's hair zeroes the sky above us, our pores tingling. His other hand traces the hard vertebrae of my nape.

13.

What I want is for her roving eye to keep still.

Instead I mimic her voice, my throat heaving with trill.

Our First Year

You ask me to hold you, if *they're coming*
now, the streetlamp pouring through
our bathroom window onto your shoulders
and unshaven face, if they'll catch you
like I've found you, curled on our tile
damp as a pea sprout.

              You've pulled your pockets
from your sweatpants, your shirt in the shower
like a fallen bat, and though I will leave you
tonight for that motel past our suburb, the one
twenty-five dollars for a smoking room
though I don't smoke, bedcover soft

as used wool but burnt through—,   I don't
know it yet, have only been eyeing the building
each time I drive home, thinking, *it's cheap*
enough for when you do it, a few nights
a week—and I don't know how I'll hold
myself there, later, watching Late Night, an actress

husking her hair from her round shoulders,
her skin gleaming like new corn, the old host
dancing to please her in some kind of thick,
hazy vaudeville, and my body at the edge
of the bed, not wanting to touch
the room's strangeness. For now,

you are so close but so foggy, walls veiled
with steam, the mirror fully clouded,
your pupils spread: your eyes full eclipses—
and I pleat at my knees to wrap around you,
because *Baby, shhh, there's nobody coming,*
Baby, there's nobody coming.

The first time you showed me, the pipe glowed
in your hand like a secret. You taught me
to pull the steel wool to two slender pieces,
how to pack the pipe, and the sliver burned
in the glass and in your hand a single spark
in the night so quietly, I could've thought

it was magic, but I was scared then too.
            I didn't know I would leave you,
sink into what you showed me, that one leaves
at night, but I'd come back at your call—:   how
many times I would learn to settle in like on an old lover
the mauve cover, trembling the cabled remote

control, waiting without knowing I was waiting
to sit out my own anger: how used I would get
to the sound of drunks serenading gritos
outside my rented room, singing to a bush,
a wrought iron gate, singing to nothing
and everyone, and my fingers pushing through

the blanket's cigarette burns, as if I were
fiddling with lace.
            Our summer will drip one day
into another, like the four walls of our bedroom
when one morning you finally come home,
your body so bent and tender, I won't

speak, will just make you paint. Who can say
what flickers privately between husbands
and wives? Each roof clamps down its own
tight gloom. We slough off on one another.
You light tapered candles, tug my hand
with your right thumb, calloused

from the sparkwheel, pull me to the porch
for romantic dinners, our voices streaming
to the street from our home in the growing
dark.   It's night now.
               You are looped on the floor
like an apostrophe, light from the window

spilling on what is naked in slats of yellow
and dark. Along tile: frogs bellow
ache, the pipe refracts a rainbow. You ask
me to hold you, and I sink to the floor, rock
our slow bodies until you quiet, not knowing
how much   my body will hold.

My Father's Family Fasts the Slaughter
to Feast the Arrival of His Bride
Ilocos, Philippines

What did she permit him to see, my mother, the first time
he brought her to the ocean—the goat, hungry—mewling
in the distance while my mother shrugged her shirtsleeve
down, her shoulder fragile in new day? Or was it her wrist
which implied the unfreckling of her forearm? The susurrus
of flycatchers . . . softened bleats of starving. A hawk is circling
closer. What do we see when we see? I can see my mother,
but never my father. His shadow darkens her arm. Her breast

sinks to a curve we three know—, and there's enough time
for hair to come loose, the popping of a button. A rat reveals
himself in the corner the way a woman tenses in and out
of light—: and my mother is coming to that point of breath-
lessness, humidity speckling her birdwing clavicles—
and the goat's hooves rustle—: above mud, before harm.

The Kiss

on Gustav Klimt's painting, 1907–1908

Do you really think if you bend
me, I will love you? You
crack my chin up, your hands
brown pigeons scheming reunion

at my cheek and temple, your jaw
cragged at the end of your thick neck
of longing. I claw onto you
as the only tree here, your

swing. I'm mad for gravity though
I'm bound, diagonally, to
you. Let me. Push from your trunk towards
the edge and my freedom. Leave me

to wither while moss weeps
in the corners, our halo liquid
as yolk, waving from our bodies' heat,
our divinity melting. My dress

blossoms loudly. You are still
wrestling me closer. If only I could
release to you my mouth just this
once and you would leave me,

but the shadows of your robe are
so haphazard. I know you will try
to smother me again. The poppies scratch. My feet
reach beyond spring.

Late September, When the Heat Releases

A sage bush flowers,
   and all night long, your skin rippled, softening

      through gaped window, the cathedral long
        with bells. Leaves crumple

       ⌒

        in the fever of water and in the morning
      you carry your cup like a letter, your blood

   heaving, your pores drying, and we open
summer, broken through the chambers of a fig—: I search your face

   ⌒

    for the hot work of bread while your thumb
      thickens. How to wind

      the lighter,
        how to sink into exhalation, how to let it all

      ⌒

       blow: out?   —and the pulse swims, rosaries
    clicking the same damned prayer, the word *intervention*

   swung from *intercession*, as if mumbling before
drug or sugar or sleep can heal us our desert's temperature, crimping

  ⌒

our bodies still. Fruit in my hand, I try to tell you
  about the scent of your diabetes, and you tell me how

    transmission lines sing when a person smokes, the singeing
      rock, lifting odored sound, —seeds swirling galaxies

              ↄↄ

            through my palm, and when many nights from other
        country, you finally call back, I say, *you're alive!*,

      and only because I can smell, I know
      I too am alive, though all night you

        ↄↄ

  sweat, dreaming the head thrown back
    in smoke, your fleecy sweetness robing

      our clutched skins. Flowers' jaws unfasten,   fumaroles
        surging purples to eat the air.

Meditations on Living in the Desert

Impulse is the pulse which threatens
to destroy us in

sand, this hurricane of paper
moths: —we followed our lovers to the desert

(their glistening backs), and now our plasma,
like static, is losing its first motion.

We are learning how to lie down quietly
each afternoon, to let

whimpers fall over us, through
the air, and through

our skin, to forget our wet mouths, their hungry
gestures, and in staying

still, only sound
throbs its course through

our stretched-out bodies, and we
are learning how to forget

how to ask for rain—

the thing is, it's not

the heat: how quickly everything changes
form, our waters

evaporating, our bodies shrinking.
It's a cactus leaf

gray as a pigeon, torn
from its stem. Not the shape

of a cactus—a body with two arms reaching
up, like a child—but the leaf,

dry in the dust, closer
to becoming less alone.

     ⌒

Mothers sleep
like corpses on tables, their faces

wounds just beginning
to make, their bodies maps, lines

drawn by men, the wind, this sun.
Women bear flowers deliriously, birds

in rain. Soldiers wait
in schoolyards now. And what matter

exists here shifts from a girl
on her knees to a girl

dying. Her throat swells
though no one will

listen. The wind can make a scream
sound like a lizard scraping

the window. Girls' shoulders
glisten with newsprint,

and our arms reach out,
though only dust grips

our palms, the lines
held there, our dumb territory.

Admit Impediments. Love Is Not Love

and snow stains the desert purple. I stand under the lintel
naked, my husband flicks through photos. This sequence, he's carried

his Canon into a temple, where the shimmering eyes
of cats: [one is scraping his tail, healed from broken, across

my shoulder; at the right edge, Thai monk gauzed orange; the libidinal
shiver of leaves like foil coins, milky gloss

of a shot.] At home, the water goes to boil
in pot. I cloud on my robe, scrub the hard ring

of the sediment of our pipes. Years
more and since

of my (un)dressing. Who can tell the diameter between
touch? The failure of my body to compete with self

as artifact. *Dawn is a damp hand*, says Susan Briante, *slipped beneath
my knee*, and under the snow, the separation of hills, black trees.

Continental Split

A business meeting in Bulacan, Philippines

You take his hand and press it to your forehead
as custom, god's voice speaking through

this clasp of his hand and your skin, your skin
sweating to feel the mosquito wading

over his knuckles and your lashes, and his wife beside you, quiet
before this man who looks like your father

with pinched-in eyes and softer lips. Your mother told you
how that hand split the continent

of this woman's skin, her back reaching out
to him in engorged and broken love, and you extend too

to set on your uncle's palms your father's land, compressed
to papers, sealed in plastic, because this is how

we declare what is ours and what isn't, what we've learned
to give away, our fibers swelling

against the wrapping, and everything
you know a secret from your mother—the words of your own

father still cutting her glottis—and your blood rising
to remember what spindles have been pricked from this man, your father,

and you, what spines you all carry, and the heat
shuddering between your wrists.

At a Party

Say your father touched you, and say you
can only remember it like a streetlight catching
the shades when, drunk at a shindig you droop
in too close to a friend, press your fingers to her
cool white arm and ask her, *are you my sister?*
Say she leaves you then, shaking her hair. The past

doesn't matter, you know that. You know this
even as the chandelier wobbles and a blonde
child sinks her cheek into her mother's
skirt, the meat, guisado, cloaking its tomato
saltiness over your skin. It doesn't matter
how after exhibits, artists (white) with Malbecs

shatter, loving one another—they disrobe
their traumas, that there was never enough
farro, or, *in college I woke to find I was no longer
home:* the chocolate cake lopsided, their eyes
dark and glassy, fingers sliding down
the stems. The soaked corners of their lips

crease to purple like the cavities of lilies. You
work, but each cycle your husband slips
on transferring the money, so you buy beans
with credit, stew ribfat from the bone.
The girl's face is hot from running, her fingers ring
her mother's thumb. You watch the buoys,

freckles bobbing her mother's neck, daughter
swimming the echo of laughing boys. You want
to pick the girl up, to curl her over your hip, but
remember Americans don't touch. On the news, clips
of farrow and Mexicans wearing surgical masks, afraid
of swine flu, their kissing mouths unkissed.

You stroke your nails over your dry, forgotten
lips. Women and men rumble the distance,
the television on but politely muted, walls
glaring with the passing of the unnamed dead. Say,
in the dark, when your husband slips his belt
through loops, you still wince, though he's never

worked his palm against you, won't even
tug your hair in bed. Light edges in
on tables, the birds of hands, in the triangles
of partygoers' eyes. The girl steams
her dumpling face into her mother's pelvis, star
sinking to nimbus. Wine tips, rims clink to form

hourglasses, and a shimmer of voices spill
their wanton yesses. Pigs stampede
the periphery, hoof to pink and rippling
body, and the black eyes, surfing masks, are mirrors
to the night. In the vise of your brown
fingers, you feel the neck of your glass break.

Panic

They are tearing out
the roof in clumps, tar plunging
the mouths of shovels, and at the donor bank they call me

a *difficult bleed*, use a scale
to measure the minimum charge given
in me. A woman breathes

down your neck, pleading you to turn on
the oven. Like this the world is always
on the verge, love

a forgotten sorrow. The better act
lost, a new roof a practice
in pollution: anxious heart,   slow burn,

and in the neighboring city seventeen more drop
their hands to their knees,   machine-gunned
at the drug rehabilitation center. This is the desert,   after

all. We are always suffering
the shape of the wind. We are always shifting where
shifting requires,   and you love me

the way a child loves his mother, which is to say the body
growing and separate. Over, and over,
you clutch at my wrist,   my breast,   bruised inner

of my elbow, our crotches a nest
of thistles, and this is how we go on
sharing passports and nightmares, the circulated

air between borders, your nipples
erect,   and the dead
around us, mineral,   and rising.

Gedankenexperiments

Thought:
  The cat is alive and dead.

  Or, how about a trial separation? How
  does the skin stretch when warmed by gas? And please, *the light*, the light now,

Conclusion:
  please. There are wives, this very minute, touching them

  -selves, their cervixes widening to door
  -men. The acupuncturist says, *Give me your palm. This won't hurt*

         ⌒

.

    at all. Border officials are building
    their electric walls, and moths hover to burn

    themselves, prisoners of the thought of light.

T:
  Meet me in México

  City. *Take your clothes off, trust me—*   Look
  how I press myself against you, your button

         ⌒

    a verb,

    becoming. We can undo

    nothing here but sheath and skin, the cat alive, her
    sister, dead. Let me, darling, trace my nail around your

C:

tooth, your gold filling. Your widening,

silky ring. You see,
this strap can slip off

           ⌒

your clavicle, seductive as idea.

A Loaf of Bread

A graduate student visits

> *The children's father stabbed and beat 38-year-old Janice*
> *Castorena, threatened to kill them if they told, and fled,*
> *police said. For two weeks, the children visited friends,*
> *made meals and kept to themselves while living in the home.*
> —October 14, 1996, AP

Jessica counts books, turns our picture frames over, folding
the dead's flat teeth to wood. She asks, *are they coming*

now? Jesus tells me to, and though I don't
really know her, I've worn her sadness

in this house. Her speckled shoulders soften
below stained glass, the nagging slant of a corner. I don't confess

how here an EMT once hunted my body for cuts, my nakedness
glowing from the Maglite, or all the strangers I've called

at night, asking questions too. Jessica drags her own shore
of voices. She says she needs to kill, snags her nails inside

her hair. And there are postcards which come
from my husband's friend in asylum which never talk of the past,

of his children in the house for two weeks, a loaf of bread
on the counter, their mother

butchered behind the bathroom door . . .   only
cursive, each shaky loop knotting toward the fringe

of god. Our chants roam throats of rooms and roses.
When she falls to sleep, I gather her silences crowding

my couch. And when she leaves, I clean
her menstrual stamp, my two hands washed in blood.

After Dinner

How do I ask Lourdes to sort the difference
between my knives? The serrated are only
for dining, the curved ones for husking
muscle from the bone, their edges hollow

-grounded, meant to phalanx at the wooden
block. She's unloading the washer, my hands
in soap and sauce, and Juárez glows
at the end of the window, the bridge

shiny as an eel. Last month, cartel thugs
hustled her husband Martín, stuck their thumbs
into his clavicles, bruised his hollows
for a teacher's bonus, while this woman, crouching

inside, counted the copper jackets sheathing
her walls. How does a woman begin
to count how many bullets are shattering
her panes? (She cupped her nervous

belly, fingered the budded navel, hummed
into the growing ear there, 1, 2 . . . 3, each
beat like systole, diastole, song made
to cleave one moment from another.) *No*

decapitations today, she tells me, though
her neighbor hung himself this week, and I dry
my hands, sponge grease from the steaming
counters. She separates each blade from the other.

The Eyes Open to a Cry

Blood moves her from the bedroom
to the bathroom, her body pulled
away from the crescent of her husband
in ended eclipse, and her toes tent
on the tile as she pleats the warm
cloth from her pelvis. Each cycle
shapes its own new stain, the irregular edges
of wetness seeping into stiffer thread,
and like this, she is still startled
to discover the appearance of her private
self: the red moon announcing her
as if her own face. This morning, the sun
has spilled circles all over the old wood
floors, slipped through the grain, and in
Juárez, seven more are dead as she washes
the blood from her panty, the field
on which the men played soccer sinking
in with human weight. She wrings
the cloth, pulls the string. Does what
she must. The wives in Juárez are used
to slumping their bellies to their knees
while the sun in El Paso kaleidoscopes
her, cleaner now, through the circles:
squinting past loud windows
and back into the soft cave of her
bedroom, where a man is breathing
into the brown right angle of his
elbow. In grass, another woman stops
breathing. The cheeks of the man she loves
are stitched into the seams of his own
soccer ball, and the women move, each
to the extension of their other; one

from blood, the other toward—both
knowing the compression of their ribs
above their cardinal hearts, the rest
of man perpetual only to the plumb
moon: and they crawl to him, raise his arms
and wade into his murky torso, blood
dampening their butterflied hips,
veil between sleeping and waking.

In Their Dark Habits

Avenida 16 de Septiembre

of skin, the soldiers watch
a girl, their machine guns propped
on cars every four feet, trained
in. She is watching them watch
her, and they are all reflection,
spectacles before the moment
of sweat, before her white shirt, red
skirt slide through the quadrants
of their sights. They are wet
with the night—everyone—as a boy
moves his finger from the cool
side of his barrel towards the hook
of his trigger. *Will they? Won't they?*,
these are questions for outsiders,
reporters from De Efe, or CNN,
the local reporters already dead
because *Will*—is for people who can
cross over and not for this girl becoming
a woman the closer she comes, her
skirt cutting itself to the grid, and her,
feeling the weight of the dampening
fabric. She's been here before. She has
been watched watching, leaving
school and entering mass, and she
is growing up through the growing dead
and before boys, always, blooming
in her body walking: its refusal
to stillness like the desert under
this city, where each grain bends
its eye to uncommon rain, and irises
carry blood, —blood she will know
as the clockwork of her body churns.

Kastanyas

Pomegranates dry in the tree and a train crosses autumn, night's parchment
pressing the crossing closer. I am calling my father on his birthday, chestnuts
splitting in the oven, the chimney suited with burns, fruit shaking their rattles.
I want to know the sleep of the compacting seed, want the Xs I've cut into each
brown shell to crimple—like hair on a man's chest—, each chestnut opening
its heart in heat. I walk the cold of my home fastening myself to gas curling
from the kitchen, and in corners: shapes of anger, each on its haunches, known
shadows. I curl my neck into each fogged silhouette, taking the depth of silence
in, having loved the knots in the bodies of men, beginning from my father,
palms dragging my breasts with mentholatum. (I've confused coolness, lifting
from pockets of air and heat as love, my pulse stopping in dark blood.) The last
    time

my father touched me, it was New Year's, I was in college, we were in Manila
on vacation, and sick with grief (we only returned to bury our own, their distant
bodies) and pneumonia, I stayed in the hotel bed, my mother and brother
in the province lighting sparklers, and my father stayed with me, watching
the pump of the ventilator, mask at my mouth pulling at my phlegm, and ever so
gently, he lifted my shirt to rub Vicks Vapo-Rub onto my chest, his hand small,
and chemical, and because I'd grown never to talk against the hard hands
of my father, how could I now speak against this softness, no shoe, no belt, only
his palm laid between the even softer fact of my breasts? He did not go further.
I did not say a word. The fireworks blew into the black square of the window,
crimson clusters, and my chest split open, my heart quiet and dark as seed.

How to Care for a Man, Withdrawing

Hold him. Warm together your skins
so his fever doesn't separate
his temperature from yours.

Press your pubis into his back,
his hair in your hand, and your other
hand washing him with a soft

cloth. Pray
his moaning will mellow as you
clutch his trunk with yours,

as water falls from your wrist
to his shoulder to your breast—:
become a bed cool

as a guava leaf in rain.
Cradle him into a child.
Let him writhe all his suffering

on you. And by morning, when he is
gnawing an apple on the balcony,
watching a woman with hairpins step

between cacti, trace your pulpy
hair down your uterus,
to the singular self

which rests there, beneath
your fingers, your hot palm,
despite all your aching flesh.

In Step

When my husband and I tried dancing lessons, we began
to realize how brittle our sacra, how we were wired

to our feet like blocky marionettes, our spines pulled down to the noncompliant
coccyges, and we braced ourselves together in squared embrace

against the clock, each sneaking our private
count of the minutes before it would be over, the male teacher swaggering

with his practiced *Elvis-cum-Saturday-Night-Fever* pout, lips
inflated over the upper teeth, and his gold chain swinging on his neck

to tint his skin, which was dark, for a white man's, and it was
6:23, more than an hour and a half of this: —him ironing my husband's palm

into my back as he danced behind us, at least two minutes more until the other
teacher would find us, tapping too, her fingers

on her wrist, *1 2 3 4—1 2 3 4*—faces of couples
sliding by and swooning, especially the young

Yoga instructor and her Philosophy professor, each just young enough
to tangle over the other like grape vines with their wrapped ballerina

blouse, their just-graying sideburns, and their *1 2 3*. We were dancing
because I'd wanted to write like Rita Dove: I had done what women do, had
    asked him to

give me this, imagining something more, moaning
one morning as I curled beside him, said *let's try it,*

as if to try would equal, simply, a quiet locking of the hips—and I was tired
of watching our dark students move our living

room tables at parties to show us the cumbia, pulling one another furiously
    and just at the edge
of their own characters developing elbows and nostrils, liquid

with each other's comings and goings, damp when I thought I had smelled
    the want
for new book contracts—something dank and sweet, because

such is the smell of knowing the world is just about to give
you everything you want—, and I was tart too entering the university

gym with my husband, holding his gray hand in my wet one and proud
that in just nine weeks we would show all our students—just sort

of dance, like surprise, like when the geeky guy in the movies
takes his glasses off, and a strip of sweat bubbles

above his lip like caviar, before he angles to the object
of his desire, who is kinky-haired and beautiful, and only slightly bitchy in the
    beginning (later

we find out she has commitment issues, she's been molested by her father,
or she's poor, she doesn't have all her papers)—but that like this, two

people should come together in rhythm over any swollen floor, matching tips,
    counting
together, *four years since we've been married, three since I sunk my womb,* maybe
    two

more to wait until my body can bear
another, and us now here before every other couple sliding

between daycare and news of beheadings, telling my husband and me as we
    stalk
our house of shoes how their children have opened their fists, or *it's time*

to go home!, and our students, dancing together and knowing
better how to hold the slick helix, our male and female

teachers both twisting behind us, showing us with their pendulous
bodies how our own should be keeping their tempo—:

Because "Some Women Are

Laramie, Wyoming

lemons," Harlan says he cares for cars instead, the plains
rising like bread from our glowing windows, Harlan's
neck blushing to heat and the women he's wrestled,
his barren limbs circling above them in a wash
of sweat and sock. We knead our common bodies
one to another, palm to bulk, and in middle
America, I sit next to a man I will never know,
taxiing, Harlan driving us this giving night. We are
three strangers in the strangeness of the talk of love,
and I am a little drunk, returning to my mother,
who stacked warm lemons on my neck. Like her, I know
how to cut from the wholeness of fruit, how to squeeze
an open body for its juice, my hand a vise,
Harlan's women softening to my fingers: the waxed
pocks of their skins, how women keep their wetness
under their bitter whites. In Georgia, we learned to drink
the watered sour, heat lightning cracking above
us, and even new housewives know how to release
from three spoonfuls a pitcher's worth, how to cut
the tart with sugar. The rind, the resistant ellipses,
are not the talk we make for men, only *Sugah, have*
some more, and there's a tart too, why, what else
could I have done with so many lemons? and we press
our sweating cups to their lips, slipping
flavor and fragrance—the shells, the containers
we broke for want of ade, cast. From the phonograph
of his front seat, Harlan's voice spins me, the man
beside me a coiling leg, and juiced, we say *lemons!* together
in the working yeast of this cab, and what unapologetic
fruit they are, leaving the smell of themselves even
after I have scrubbed my hands free from them, my wrists

having pushed men to drink, *oh, Sugar*, and I want more
than anything now to call out for my mother,
who could roll into a room with the oval of her uncut
self, who could press her palm hot against my chest
as I breathed. We exhale our imbibed spirits out
to glass, wrapping ourselves in smoke.
Harlan chews a Nicorette each time he tries to break open
a woman and she serves him only lemons. Night
is moving us through another coming winter
and we laugh quietly now to the pressure, each coming
to the cool center of our single selves, and each pressing
the other away from our own opposing bodies, where
we are drifting to our separate and yellowed hallways,
to perfume, the persistence of our missing women.

Displaced Women's Blues

Expelling a groan to siphon pain, women cry softly
in toilet stalls, lengthening their emptying. The body erupts
to loosen what it cannot contain, like a mother bleeding
from her ear to call her daughter home. The phone clicks its uneven

whine, lengthens its emptying. Bodies erupt
in earthquakes, bagyos, tsunamis. We call our old countries, flattening
our ears to strain up our lost homes. The phone clicks our uneven
survivors out. And mothers slip children their first bacteria, pulsing

nipples to gumming mouths. In bagyos, tsunamis, we call for our old countries
     flattening
to concrete. A mother drops an ocean from where
her daughter survives, and mothers slip children their first bacteria,
milk microbed for another soil. A child's tooth breaks

on concrete. Mother drops an ocean. From our
lips, longing weaves a chainmail of ghosts,
microbes netting the soil. A child's tooth breaks through,
white signaling separation. We bury the native language with Mother's

puffed lips, longing and weaving, but a mail chain of ghosts
comes, red and blue, via international post. We smudge the white letters
signaling separation, bury the native language. Into our mother
-bodies, our sons burrow their dark wet heads, though women's regrets

come, red and blue, via international post. We smudge the letters
of our names. The sky sings in sudden summer hail.
Our sons burrow their dark wet heads. Women's regrets
grow on hoary ankles, black as pansies, secretive

as Spanish names. The sky sings in summer hail
as a woman moans in a tiled public space,
sound the residence of her throat. We fountain
black pansies, cotton compressing our ankles.

Women moan in tiled public spaces
to loosen what we cannot contain. We bleed,
sounding our residenceless throats. Our bodies fountain,
and we cry softly, expelling a groan to siphon the pain.

You Say You Can't Sleep

For B——, my lost friend

again, the train crying miles away drips your walls and doorjambs, so
you squeeze / your body from forehead to toe, rippling each muscle to
submission: / contraction, the work of rest. Only you still find yourself

thinking too hard about the conductor—though in Tai Chi they say
learn quiet, receive / and offer—is his mother still alive?, what is he
wearing?, is he picking his nose just now, / and why the faux pas with
the crusting nostril

when everybody picks and fingers anyway? You open your hands to
the night, / your edges abandoning themselves. You say out loud you
won't do it again, you won't / call the beautiful boy who brings you
meth like an offering,

crystal glittering his shaking palm. No, not tonight. Focus / on your
own exposed hands, your fingers cupped up like the spokes of a crown,
the folds / streaking your palms, your skin lifting to sky. It stunned you

the first time a man kissed you, the taking of lips, the way you jumped,
then / crumpled, man into man: how in him, you learned to surrender.
In the desert / heat, he taught you to understand the entrance

of pain aligned with sex, and finally you understood women. He was
married and so / were you. You washed his mouth carefully from
yours, your tongues releasing / like a handshake ending: contraction,
then distance.

Tonight, you are alone as you have been for years, but the train
impresses itself / like the lights of this city, showering shadows on your
moulding. You try to remember / the smell of your mother. *Ice*,
incinerated, hisses through

glass, and the thing you like best is the sound, husky rush through the throat / of a pipe, precision of your own breath inhaling, your loud lungs, your ears / flattening to electricity—: then nothing. You sink

back, imagine your pillow a lover. Remember to squeeze / your muscles. How odd, to have so many tricks to sleep, when on boys' faces, rest seems always / possible. A falling body's velocity remains constant

unless impelled on by external force, which is why in dreams you love / the sensation of falling. The stillness, as if, if you raised your hand to your face, you would not / find it there. A body on another moves

equally and oppositely: and when you kiss, you push and fall back, and you breathe / in, hold, then release. You miss the sound of your mother's feet. The soles indenting / wood as the wood indented grains

on her, roughening her skin to cracks. The body opens so easily what the heart / cannot. Tonight, you cannot. If only sleep would take you before the phone crawls / to your palm. People have learned to hide

the fluids spilling their cavities from others: blood, spittle, mucus. And you / have learned to hide too, your body stiffening and slackening, your mind wandering / hallways, searching for the heel of a dream you knew

once, before this unbearable blue of your room, the square glowing light of your i / -phone. You remember the hard sapphire of mass, fingers compressing a wafer / to your tongue. Your pillow lingers mussels. Light

is so much more difficult than sound. Through glass, the city flashes shadows / into your bedroom, hard architecture, each joint meeting the other in the dark. / You cannot sleep, and perhaps a hit, just one

would help you—a chemical rest is better than no rest—this uneven beating / of your heart, your million alveoli stretching the hot shell of your chest, and your soft / body sparkling on the sheets, open as a clam. When a boy touches you, you feel the vertical knock of each vertebra, a charge / running your meninges, burn lurking the synapse. When you touch him, you feel / you love him as your mother loved you, you are taking care

of him, and he would sleep on the street if you don't call him now, because / this is the desert, there are clots of boys and men migrant on the border, / their mouths breaking in the night, and the air

dry as paper, crackling from Juárez. You cannot sleep, not knowing where the boy / you guard will sleep. The air is heavy and you contract, receive the night / spilling your body, your hands shaking with offering.

Thai Massage

In the dark room he asks me
to change where we have to
bow below the ceiling, coughing
while he draws the sheet hung
to save my modesty, though
I have none to save. I peel off
my wet dress for pants thin
as the pillowcases I slept on
as a girl in Georgia, the purple
tie-dye ballooning my pelvis,
and I knot the remaining cloth
at my navel, fold the sheathing
I arrived inside, seams filled
with smoke, city, into a sharp
black square at the corner
of the single mattress. I can see
his body moving quickly, quietly
lighting candles behind the cot
-ton: divided, we both know not
to speak. This is the last trip
I'll take with the one I still call
my husband, this man and this
room now a bought hour
of silence from the silence of
my body walking behind another
in Bangkok, and I pleat myself
into the center of the bed, my
calves under my thighs, palms
sweating the lap, the way Asian
women know to wait. He senses
my pinned posture and pulls
the twin sheet back, and for

the first time I see him beyond
instruction, or introduction, how
the small hoods of his eyes drip
into his smooth high cheeks,
his tendonous neck and clavicles
rooting to a person more furtive
than my own. He asks me where
I hurt, everywhere. But more
at my neck and lower back,
because I won't ask this stranger
to cup the cone of my caged
heart. The springs depress
where he has sunk in to hold
me, his chest at the hump
of my spine, my hands in
his, our fingers entrenched.
He says of our shared, colored
skin *same, same*, and I say *sawat
dee ka* because I do not know
how to use the language past
gratitude—my accent broken,
tiger balm spiriting his pores,
and his breath at my neck, the two
candles hunkering blue light
in the corner, and somewhere
below, banned from this dark
room and in the laboring street
is the one who's forgotten
to touch me, a man framing
in telephoto the smoky arms
of women frying chicken over gel
gas, and the foreheads of girls
hacking durian, their temples
shining, bent to the million
spines at each green shell, their

steel knives unstringing such
soft yellow fruit. Still to come
is a grief so large it will shape into
an estranged and swollen face
cursing me at the next party, our
future folding into our past, wine
staining our hands, our lips.
The sun drops, conspires
to further the darkness of this
blued room, where candles are
shivering in secret. The fan
whirs. The man embracing me
squeezes our four hands, and I
understand the gesture to trust
him. He swings me, cracks my back.

Bodies, and Other Natural Disasters

Six Jewish women are entering a bath, their breasts
the only parts of their bodies fat enough to rise, and the camera
man, head down, remembers: *the old woman was chanting
a prayer.* Cut scene. Now the men have been forced
to bathe, and for lack of breasts we can see the hooked
ribs, the canyoned stomachs, each shank delicate

as a cockerel's, and their beards curling down like the hair
spilling above their soft, compliant penises. Each scene
has been well-scripted: bathing, funerals, circumcisions, each
practice of life in the ghetto commissioned for documentation,
and it would seem like a movie, if only there weren't corpses

being walked over, that same group of people asked to cross
the camera tiredly over the dead. The point is for the people
to look heartless. Never mind who laid the bodies
down, or who is directing the living behind
the camera's eye. They are faceless, free
of noise as the women and men walking now, or washing

and weeping, the Wehrmacht inked only in their wet
eyes each time these unpracticed actors look, accidentally, right
into the lens. It's night. My dog has screwed his body
into my husband's foot. Here, the untouchable blue
of sifted light rises, like skin straining

to a church's windows. I am watching each fragment
of film silently, the captions black tags of context, though
the two-pound boy (the cameraman calls him an actor) held
quietly, his skin marbled like a ham, is context enough. The quick
neat blade, blood dark as chocolate after. I never learn
if the boy lives, though I really should

ask, lives after what? Survive the circumcision, suffer working
the graves: your uncle, brother, the girl who hid crackers
in her waistband whom you could have loved, if only
her jaw wasn't cymbaling her teeth now, her face
in the skull barely visible. Ashes still fall in the Philippines

from Pinatubo, sinking to desks like dandruff. We watched
the powder drifting above us, thought at last we were
witnessing snow. We were kids, what did we know. We only held
our palms open, crying for our mothers to look, look.
In Miyagi, the tide arches like the eyebrow of an angry
woman. Walls break, people run, and in the middle of this,

I imagine a girl, also baring her expectant palms, her life
line, love line, crevices seeking water. I have woken without
the sun, only these fragments of film strobing to light
the different edges of our room: dog here, tail of a cat cresting
like a wave before it drops, with the rest of its body, off

the bed. I cannot see the entirety of my husband's shape,
only the rising and falling of his rest. What passes above
me, I cannot name, though I recognize it partly
as grief, partly as thirst, and in my soreness, I remember
my mother stitched secret pockets to my pants. She hid coins,
notes, pressed the paper and cold circles to my skin. My mother

practiced safety, taught me to fear each dark
sedan pulling near the sidewalk, so when my brother dropped
with fever in Stamford, I laid his head on my lap, refused
every neighbor who tried to lift him up. Memories jolt us
in the marrow of night like thirst. *Take care*, we say, *be aware*

and wary, tug the latex tightly down the tip, and in
Chartres I traced the impossible spirals, for how could
such builders have taken care? My mother walks the emptied

rooms in the house of my puberty, dragging her fallen
leg. Her husband and children have left. *It's just
your dad works so much*, she says, Easters, Christmases,

Saturdays and Sundays. She whispers to me the few
times I call, pressing her cell to her mouth, those lips
which dripped syllables to ease my bruises, and the odor
of Vicks weighting the dark, my mother
snuck from her husband's bed. We call now to mix

stories of cooking and cats, our throats soft to talk
at all, and when I travel out of country, she knows not
to listen for my ring. The last time I saw
her, I was taking her home to bury her brother. Our women
wailed like the ocean, though we never saw the water
beyond the plane. Bodies stack upon bodies, the tide

withdraws its claim. She says, *mag-ingat ka, anak,
the* Wall Street Journal *says the drug war's crossed over,
don't you know minamahal pa rin kita?*, and I keep
my borderland from her, say nothing of our yielding
necks. She must see the mounding dead here

like a movie as I screen now these fragments, the fingers
shucked their whorls, the slow collection of teeth. She turns
the gas knob off, twelve times. Then each light switch,
a mother's dozen. She has learned to take care
so carefully, her eye twitches with each winding
danger. And there should be danger, for all we've done.

Cut back to the women bathing: the old woman's lips,
two bees. Their breasts, still beautiful, are sickled
as waning moons, and the grays of their bodies shift
as they sink, deeper, their skin. In the middle
of night and rising water, all we have is prayer.

For Want of Water

an ant will drown himself, his body submerging
    into ease, his mandibles, head, antennae, baptized. How lovely
        to lose your senses to the cup of your want. A boy
            drags his mother's body across the desert, her fluids rising
                to heaven in order to quench her skin. How divine
                    her body must have looked, clutched at the ankles, her
arms reaching out in exultation, her head stippled in rings
    of sand and blood as he walked with her, slowly, her fallen
        and moving shape the fork of a divining rod, her body shaking
            with each of his steps, and for water, shaking to find
                that deep and secret tributary. I have dreams of letting go
                    of water, of waking my lover to a bed of my urine
as my brother did to me, his thin limbs shaking to discover
    the shame of his inside self. And what did we know that to have
        an inside wet enough to free was luxury? The boy
            walks with his mother—he is only thirteen—the age I learned
                to stroke on the toilet the blood off my fingers, and he can-
                    not cry, because to cry would mean the waste of his own
wetness, to cry would mean to stop, to think, to differentiate
    the liquids moving down his face, to cry would mean
        to cry, so he goes on, and—this is a common story, the boy
            is not a boy now but every boy we have ever known—people
                find him, they help him to lift his mother onto their hands,
                    their necks, they lift her to their own dark and desperate
dryness, and they make it, yes, when they make it over the border
    to a mall parking lot, they lay her down, they fall with her
        body as a clump of bodies behind a city
            dumpster, and people make calls from behind windows, not
                to the immigrants with the dying core, but to the police, who come
                with their handcuffs and call her *dead*. No. To call

would be to give her life a name. Roundness to where there are
    now only angles. To call would be to remember all
        the other times that he has called for her, and the boy plugs his
            ears, shakes his head, doesn't know that he cannot physically
                produce tears anymore—such thirst can rid us of these symbols—
                    only that now there are mouths around him calling other names
as men run and other men give chase, because how much do you need
    to give up in order to stay? a boy? a mother? your land and inner
        land? Nothing. Nothing can be given, and he will remember
            nothing as he sits in a cell waiting for his sister to come to release
                him from his cellular pain. He will only remember water, that want
                for the clouds to let go their rain, and how seeing

them dropping, he kept pulling forward, their bodies steady towards that
                                dark, uneven line.

III

Rose is a Rose is a Rose is a Rose

Autopsy:

In sockets, combs of sticky eggs
like tapioca. Receding gums. You say, go

closer, under the cotton, press your fingers
down, spreading his skin, the bullet holes sprouting

his cheeks, black beans. You butterfly him,
forehead to pubis. My hands grow

shadows, my palms pink capes over
the density of his blackening body.

How we come to smoke:

I turn my hands over the light,
      shell of flesh, bulb obscured
           through translucent bone. I walk

          into a room where a man is
      sleeping. I walk out,
and my mother dies. Water

              hammers behind the walls and in my knees.

High, high, high:

Jigsaw of light. Tripitas.
                A wedding ring.

Spin the sparkwheel over flint, and the gas valve opens. Air singeing
                                      the pharynx.

A woman with teeth laughs, jiggles her necklace.

Wire hisses
                and my heart hummingbirds.

Autopsy, Juárez:

Slowly you stitch a Y, closing the cadaver.

Tale, two cities:

Electricity spits from fallen poles and you pick
from a plate of bones. I suck on an intestine. The sun

sinks the horizon, light hatching hills. Women
calling names through the dark. El Paso's star

burns a mountain. A moth hinges his wing.

El Paso, and Juárez is smoking again.

High and low:

I click the lighter, sink   back, let this all blow.

Crack rock, a hard place:

A tooth under the gum, impressions of space, radiant weight.

A dragonfly pistons from your fingertips and when you wake, my pillow's
a shroud—: the smell of your mouth lingers.

We drive downtown, watch people cross over

the bridge. A woman steps into our car, speaking our common language.

At the corner store, a shelf full of glass tubes filled with roses, bright
suspensions of silk.

We pull out the roses, pack the glass with rock and brillo.

                              Our necks arching long in smoke.

Autopsy, us:

You sleep with a reflected

me. I watch us through isinglass, our

limbs filmy, gelatinous. I reach in

to unclasp the pulmonic valve, and our tongues

reach for each other like clouds

visiting themselves in puddles.

Drug war:

Bury him in Spanish.

    Bury his rifle and all the bees.

        And bury me my knees, drowning to ecstasy.

How we love to score / (buying glass pipes at the barrio store):

We say it's the last, we say just one more.
We say the war we're not responsible. We say

we won't. Then we pull roses, petals leaking
thread, red blossoming their glass tombs.

IV

Sea Change

Morning, and light seams
through Juárez, its homes like pearls, El Paso

rippling in the dark. Today I understand
the fact of my separate body, how it tides

to its own center, my skin crumbling from thirst
and touch. The sun hangs

like a bulb in corridor: one city opening
to another. When did my heart

become a boat, this desert the moving
chart of my palm? And when did pain invert

the sky to glaucous sea, each home on each hill
rocking? I would give my lips

to a soldier if only he would take them
as sextant, our mouths an arc, my tongue

the telescoping sight between. Below
such light, the measure of boys

swimming cobbles, their stomachs
dripping wild stamen. See

how they are clutching to their guns
like lovers, as if the metal could bear them.

Morning, and still in umbra, my dog
and I walk, her tongue a swinging rudder.

At the Symphony: 7 Things I Wish I'd Told You

I.

Such sustained silences always

in rows, defining us from listening
to staging—desire stringing

the gut between.

2.

We learn in sound to preserve
a solitary dwelling, but your name pools

in the single violin as if to speak

it could bring us home.

3.

Voice clings to a throat
of wood. In the highest

pitch I can hear

4.

                          the jasmine, suffering

night's guillotine, its white petals dividing
my black hair: the flower splayed there.

5.

In halls, I lost you

as I lost our daughter, your amniotic
bodies swimming darkly.

6.

Bass extends footsteps.

Drums signal an end of war.

7.

And if only across the velvet
your hand could have

crossed that soft gulf.

[Rules for Behaving on an Airplane]
& *Simultaneous Monologue on Your Separate Grief*

[We are not supposed to talk. The shell holding
us, thin. Cities square their patterns through
fogged windows, and the whites of clouds rise

like sorrow.] *Today your father is dead, and you*
send me text messages, broadcasting what cannot
be said, or undone, a phone's screen such liminal

space, and—[In this statued corridor, our tired
bodies, mouths slung open like night
windows. I gather my elbows, folding my need

to touch another, in.] *sleep, or the state of reception,*
uneven, have kept us from connecting
one telegraph to the next. What good can my flying to you

do when you park outside the sealed shutters
of your father's house? One body can never
account for another missing body. My breasts

are dry as stones, I know, and even if I sling
your head there, you will smell bleach in place
of my skin, —you will memory to the circles

we darkened by mop and water, swiping his hall
-ways for passages towards "livable" . . . [Pass
-engers, we pretend not to see the loosely socked

foot, that tenuous dance before the lavatory
door, and we rein our coughs into our chests:
microtensions of politeness.] *and those floors*

will no longer collect razorblades, wooden
signs, or photos, stick to his slow, forgetting
steps: the late nurses slipping pills, disappeared

like white ghosts. A gathering of milky faces,
piles of Polaroids [I want to say, "Husband,
I'll be there soon," but here I must maintain radio

silence, and on planes time continues
until the first act of descent.] *you've sifted, searching*
for a moment when you children wore

creased smiles. Husband, your father is dead... :
[And in this holding pattern of the cramped
body, I wait for the break of our common air—]

Last Photograph of My Mother Laughing

The one in the book after this, you're in the Louvre, whiter
and colder than Venus. It will be winter, your hands

in veins, your lips tight as marble. But now, it is spring
in Manila, Jim Croce's voice is wrapping against

an aging purpling sky where a seam of your hair puffs
up—, nebulous perfection. You've placed your hand

on your hip in young, flirtatious refusal. One wrist steels
with a watch so big, it's halfway to falling, and your arms are

plain and hairless enough to turn into a statue's missing
limbs. Gallery mother, swing of my heart,

you're standing above three black-haired sisters
who as I look at you there, are dead.

The investigative report says "dark sky, calm wind"
in Louisiana when Jim gazed out the plane's window,

morning sticky with haze. Your city aches in the corner.
And your mouth breaks so cleanly across the sky.

When in Solitude, the Surprise of Morning

Gas ignites, a pin point
of light, and pigeons shift, calling

their hurt behind
walls. The cathedral laments another

hour, and just like that we turn
from morning to night, night

to morning. We are unfolding
ourselves to nearly imperceptible

changes, silent as synapses, and the bread
refuses its rise, froth spilling

the edges. When does the word *divorce* become
a sound? What cells

do we slough, still, together, in emptying
rooms? My skin has failed

me, my beauty this falling breast, and a cello
strains herself like a wife

calling her husband home. Like this
the sky comes to erase all

stars, and like this,
the phone rings, its voice untaken.

Leaving the University Gym

September, and the great stillness
of moonless night and cooling air, the city
in blue pockets in the hills, and just
under your hands, the current
of what's forgotten. All week long, while
you were running, or reading, your forefinger
blurring the type, one season was slipping
into another, as lovers weave themselves
across a bed, odor of yeast
from the beer bread lifting through
the oven, the dog's pad cracked, and in
class, you were watching one student
blink at another. *There's a time
to believe in love*, you'd thought,
watching her rub her arm hair, and him
shift in his shirt, *but then you believe all
things end*, and you'd tried so carefully
to explain what Marilyn Hacker meant,
how we "wake to ourselves, exhausted,
in the late," before you thought better
about it, staring down the rows, and cited
the *fused limbs* and *raised unlettered power*
instead, the poem's words comets' tails
on blackboard. Now, you are finally leaving
campus, content this time your heart
has bettered the howl for sugar, your body
hot from the work of itself, when you push
through the glass door into fall—

and you remember a draft which was
just like this once, when, past
the dorm curfew, Tim was clutching
your elbows beside a lake, the air cricket
-thick, Cassiopeia encrusted in her collar.
There is no loneliness as knowing. Years

later, when you were drunk yet again
at Le Lido, swimming the booth,
the waiter—cloudy in his captain's suit—sat
with you. The gold-enameled dancer
was still mounting her white horse. He poured
the champagne. You sipped it softly.
Their muscles erupted into the shivering
other as they strutted circles against
the stage, animal and woman, and you were
grateful no one said a word. How
could you have named the chill
of her breasts, the terrible hot fur?
It was that gift of silence which happens
between strangers, out of country. Then
you'd walked home, tall cathedrals
bristling in the baubles of their unrung
bells. You'd turned your collar up
against the coming cold as you turn
up your jacket now, surprised
by the suddenness of the season
(or your own inattention to the small
shifts), your breath crystal in air—
and each stripe marking separation
down the asphalt is lamped
and glistening, eerie as snow, solstice
certain as the short drive ahead, to when
you must walk up to your dark, quiet
house, sink your key into the lock.

Tuesday Night in Montparnasse

. . . These nights / I harbor a secret pity for the
moon, rolling / around alone in space without / her
milky planet . . .
                                        —Dorianne Laux

A man outside a café is putting his gloves on slowly, tugging
the leather over his wrist, and he is, perhaps, waiting for me
to put my knife and fork down, to come out from behind
my FACTS ABOUT THE MOON and slurried plate, because we have

been alone this dinner, watching that couple toast teaspoons.
We have watched them from our swampy corners, sugar
speckling her lips while she stirs her coffee, the oil-haired man
stirring too. Tonight, he will hold her cleanly in the dark

bowl of his pelvis. She will rest herself there, clutching his kinks,
whispering *darling*. Strangers, eating alone together estranged in
old cities are complicit in the nuances of other strangers' loves—
we want to come together tugging our guardedness on

like wool scarves, our tongues coated with the unsayable,
and this German man daring me one reflective iris from under
the brim of his cap is watching me watch the screening
of his hairless pulse. Flurries collect between us. I do not know

if I understand enough to leave the warm place too, to leave
where I have robed my heart in whisky, to step to the other side

of the glass just long enough to ask him for a cigarette, and then
a light, or just to gesture to the lovers, as if to ask, *can you believe*
it? Tonight, the glass divides me from that woman sitting
with gold lettering on her forehead, her black hair heavy on

the outsider's chest, and when he closes his buttons, her face
falls through his fingers. My mouth ripples leather. Dorianne
says she harbors a secret pity, and though I know
she means the moon, I want to believe it's me she's thinking

of, growing further from myself, because now he is stepping
away and my reflection is shrinking, the moon of his wrist
eclipsed in window's winter—and I bow my head down
to read: *alone in space without* and *Forget us . . . After all*

we've done. I tug my pork through the gravy, work
my knife down soaking flesh. She croons, *you can't help it*
either, you know love when you see it, and under
the silver, my plate sings, the hot ceramic cracking.

Moment in Storm

Photograph within a photograph: on Douglas Yates's photo of a snowstorm in the context of Yutaka Takanashi's "Golden Gai Street, Bar Hakata"

Snow obscures a window and emergency happens
like this, the windshield wiper clicking and her mouth
petaling open—:
                    In a photograph by Yutaka Takanashi, a bar is just this
shy of a chanteuse crooning "Dream A Little Dream of Me,"
the catalogue of eight tracks pulled from recklessly, cigarettes half
-smoked, the whisky still warm, only no one's there, all
these clues of people and no one's there, you can almost still hear
the city sirens. But then there's the matter of the camera

as observer, because in order for this glimpse before apocalypse
to exist, someone *had* to be there, someone lingered, and you
begin to wonder if you too would've stayed with your city
wailing around you, the neon signs hissing and all the precious liquors
in glass, quivering. The enemy, flying above with his bomb, is
no longer relevant, he's too far away, and you are dreaming
this scenario just as driving, the blizzard begins to take over
your sight. You compress the brake. The road refuses

revelation, and your wife is beginning to sing to calm
the children shuffling their cramped backseats. It's these times
when glass condenses that Ella Fitzgerald fogs in your ear,
your wife's voice heavy with *stars shining up above you,* her
meter steady as the arc of the wiper sweeping water, *night
breezes seem to whisper I love you* and the sky strings its purple
cords, because now your wife is really getting into it, you can see
her teeth in the window as the song takes over her, *sweet dreams*

'til sunbeams find you . . . yes, and in the windshield, red smears: cars
going, or a signal to stop, and all your reflected faces wrinkling
into snow banks, condensation of winter and breath flat
against the glass, and you can feel the storm taking over
your driving to that crushing violet sky—

                                             your wife's face
familiar and watery, because she cannot stop responding to the call
of this world, she is the kind who in the middle of emergency will
linger, a siren, singing wildly, *escape now, dream a little dream of me.*

Marking. Connecting: Between Going and Stopping,—

An exclamation mark is like laughing at your own joke.
—F. Scott Fitzgerald

We never let go. Ever. Even with punctuation. It's frightening.
—Chris Lowe

Death is a set of parentheses, fat at the sides, a heaving hush
between. Orpheus plucked the round bracket of his lyre, calling
his wife from Hades, her torso arcing to hear him. How he sung
her. How he could not bear but to look, one last time, to see
if she was following. And how the Styx dissolved her face

to ellipses, the spaces of their longing growing the horizon.
Each day I hear Orpheus knocking himself on the head,
limping around his rent-controlled apartment stuttering, *how
could she escape me?* How can a lover's shape so simply slip
through evened dots? In dreams, he raises his hand

and is squinting, is shielding himself the sight of her corpse
as question mark, already losing her calves. He walks to her,
though sometimes he's wading and uttering promises: *I'll take off
my socks, we'll quit the HBO,* Orpheus imagining himself godlike
and free from black argyle, swimming above her white and sinking

form. But by now she's always semi-colonal, risking going
full colonal, and when he reaches into the water, he claws up
hair, a string, a porcelain crown. So many nights he has surfaced
only her remnants, his fingertips have wrinkled permanently.
He's scraping his nails through his comb-over, and I am muttering

to him now, *maybe next time*. I offer him a bowl of rice, knowing
he won't stay. He just wants me to understand he might be going
on a big trip soon, will I watch over his place. *From those Ching
Chong kids—and no, Lady, I don't mean you*. His hands a pair
of brackets. His scalp pitches pink quotations through the silver.

He could've been handsome, before all this. *Pops*, I say, *stay
awhile!*, but the Blue Bell's already melting. He'd never meant
to pause so long. I stop wringing my towel, give him
a cheeky kiss. Orpheus sings goodbye for now, forgets
to tell me he'll be back soon, *just wait*—only hefts his paper

sack, its crinkling stains: the man a hunching ampersand. And
down the flickering hallway, his feet heavy with exclamation.

Old Beds and Hollywood

The day I left my house
for another home, the sky
was pink. I could hear
the first train or the last
in the distance. As if it was
any other morning, I'd made
my bed in my home office where
I'd been sleeping to feel
in my body, too, alone—
my husband snoring behind
our old bedroom, and I
stepped around his breath
the way as a girl I used
to step from my room along
my father's expirations,
heel to toe, each arc of each
of my feet muscling to
the next catch and release
of his nose and diaphragm,
my body sliding out only
at each extended blow
and whimper. My father
slumbered so loudly I could
never hear my mother's
sleep, and even at night,
with his forearm strung
over the flattened bridge
of his nose and his forehead,
all joists trembled to him
from behind the plaster,
my father's tempo leading
me slowly down the hall
to his office, where, encircled

in the blue glow of his small
T.V., I watched old scenes:
Annette Funicello folding
an orange sweater, singing
"I'll never change him," or
Doris Day on the party line,
the screen split to their two
pillows, and at the left, Doris:
her cheeks more gauzy
than the gown ruffling
her pink wrists, the phone
bigger than her round, flushed
face. I liked to lay on
my stomach as I watched
them, the women with hair
brushed and brushed, even
in bed, the delicate gates
of their lips as each resisted—
and the way too the men in
those films grabbed the women
who were insulting them,
until words turned in
-to struggle, then transformed
to desire—and I could
feel the carpet against
my shirt, my father still
snoring past the dark under
-seam of the door, my hands
in my thick hair, guessing
how a man might grip
my ears—and the films always
seemed to end at kiss, even
if there was a wedding after,
or if husband and wife
were later seen smoothing
the sheets of their separate,

twin mattresses—: it wasn't
the home which mattered,
nor the chamber, but *the kiss*,
that moment I imagined was all
a woman wanted, couldn't
live without, his body surfing
her body under, until hers
turned to the dark and foamy
water beneath his larger,
insistent wave, until there
was nothing left of her
but what rolled into him,
the current of his body
crushing, and overwhelming,
the gulf of his pull deaf
-ening as an oncoming train.

School Terrorist Exercise, 2005
Sapulpa, Oklahoma

Exactly after the end of prayer, the principal
asks us to crouch and slide our bodies into the spaces
below our desks, our elbows angling from the metal
legs and their rusted feet, to duck the wads of gum
that generations of second graders have patiently
compressed with their tongues and then

their molars, and finally their busy fingers, the pink
and yellow cities hanging above us, such pliancy
stretched like telephone wires, each piece
trying to string back to the mouth who molded
it. This could be fun, and certainly the children
laughing in front of me think so, a chance to start

our lessons with the fluorescents still off, dark morning
burning through the window. For me this is work,
this trying to silence their escapable mouths, one
hand shielding my head and the other jutting
my index finger again and again against my lips.
What if a man, M-16 tucked in, his thumb just

on the button of a nearby bomb hears us, one giggle
enough to push him from the hallways and into
our classroom, a single sound enough to trigger
the flashes which destroy us, our faces brightening
then dissolving, and all these cinderblocks fall
to flatten our desks and our sneakers? Part of me

thinks this is ridiculous, another part half hopes
to see his face squinting through our wired
institutional window, eclipsed by the construction
paper we teachers had been asked to tape
over our doors, which we did, as the children scattered
in, as if a square of blackened paper could save us

from hurt. I imagine him winding the knob, the black tip
of his barrel announcing his hands, how I might try
to squish him between the frame and steel door,
having all my life huddled in hallways, on planes, having
exercised such different impending dangers. Here,
Dhahran, or Atlanta, no matter the city my body's in,

there is always a possible fire, quake, or worse,
and officials teach us to lace our fingers tightly
onto our neck bones: that if we can just kneel
patiently, steady our foreheads to the tile, an act of god
against the other acting god will happen. On CNN,
my mother and I watched the Khobar Towers crumble

where our friends in Saudi slept, each level of living
space falling one on top of another in the middle
of rising sand and smoke. All the calls long
distance, the wringing of hands when we found
a volcano in our homeland had ruptured.
My mother searched each of the passing faces

on the bulbed screen as if every gray, caked oval could be
her own, the announcers busy saying: *devastation, Pinatubo,*
those poor people in the Philippines, how unfortunate that
exactly at 1:42 pm Tropical Storm Yunya was also passing
through, officials are trying to evacuate the villagers now
but tephra, *that's a mixture of volcanic ash and water, Pat,*

is raining: So, even if hugging your knees to the sound
of Lola singing each Hail Mary worked, if for such
recitation the right terrain gave way
to guide the lava away from your home, all you needed to do
to die was to step outside and breathe. Emigrants kiss
their rosaries, thinking, *it wasn't us*. The exiled sink

to carpet, imagining themselves coupling, ash to ash,
finally home again. Today I shush each laughing second
grader, stare down Cheyenne Sweeney loud with spit
bubbles, my mother would've said she was *making rain*.
In college, watching a plane and the first building compress
to ruined accordion, I left my T.V. to run into the city,

searching for someone to hold. The boy next to me
lost his cross in the evacuation; I should've helped him
look. In disaster, every ward has a plan of escape,
how best to spill from the wreck, and in schools we stop, drop
and fold, arranging, arranging our limbs for the siren.
In Oklahoma, tornado speakers flare across the green,

unforgiving land. We crouch under our desks, our makeshift
bodies contracted. Cheyenne's lips glisten, blowing
rain, her bubble growing then popping, saliva expanding
from her mouth pink and wet with breath, and we wait,
holding ourselves until the speaker clicks, for the voice above
to say: *good morning, you can come out now, it's over.*

V

What Is Broken

A cricket's surrender when I open
your jaw. Each of our languages, missing

translation. Density of the radio tower,
cut by night, and your son's scalp,

needing stitches. Every marriage, its mis
-carriages. Lightbulb. The canary palm

scissored by moon. My heart, and each moving
box I've shut, unpacked. My oven, missing

its starter. Tea cup
on the counter. Low moan lost

from the distant dog—perhaps the one I'd fed once—
then, your mouth, back

of a spider. The code, parsed and morsed. Skin from
splinter. Moment you first held him, before

words, before hunger. The want
to want again. A single cry made whole, through

touch, with silence. Your hair breaks
into the million stars as you tell me your father

-stories. The dry planes of our fingers,
splitting to reach another.

Before Dawn

Almost December, and the house stiffens, trains
calling their distance, each car sweeping some brace
of memory by, and coffee loosens its warmth
to my chest. A boy steams up from my childhood
and Connecticut: he's bent over the bench at an old bus
stop, his breath expellant, and his left hand cups over
his morning work while his right gathers a night
-crawler, the pale moons of his fingernails severing
the worm to two. The rest of us kids are gawking,
bubbling to noise and smearing our sniffles into
mittens, but the writhing body—bright as fire
in this boy's hands—is still alive, we are shocked
at its life, the way one body can unlatch in the hands

of another. Dawn hesitates in the beak of a clicking
bird, and the memory of your stomach swims
from the sheets in its glistening whiteness. They say there
are more moths this year than any other, we are
swatting them from our hair, our eyes, and I know
when I unlock my door I should be disturbed
at their insistence, their electric fluttering, but I have
held my arms too over a light, willing to burn
for the sight of that one incandescence, bulb signaling
the presence of someone at home, porch morse-coding
messages through the fingers pulling its switch. If
I dialed you now, would I remember your voice,
its pattern of soft parts, flushed stresses? The boy

from my first American winter is still cupping
his palms over that worm, his breath hard jet, and all
the windows of home cloud over. Our mothers sweep
their shadows over the front desert step. If we could only
return to the moment before separation, move

the bristle back to brick, glutinous half to vermicular
half, your hand again to my hand . . . all the porches
of this district could turn on like watchtowers, our half
of the city sink into light. Schizophrenic morning
splits: white, and the changing dark—necessary
suicide to shift into a day, *der schwer gefasste ent*
-schluss, and we enter our days heavy with dreamed
terrors—after showers, water streaming our hot elbows.

⌒

Es hob

sich eine Woge heran im Vergangenen, oder

da du vorüberkamst am geöffneten Fenster,

gab eine Geige sich hin   as I yield to you now at this window,

                              particles of silica suspended

                    in pane. In Paris, I spent a winter listening

                         for the fall of a boot, the stairs

              cracked by carriers of corpses, and we build cities

                         one above another, entombing our pasts:

Lampshade.

White archway. Torn fringe, gold

ring resting between cobbles.

Before Google, a Nietzschean signed his last letter to me *amor
fati*—and standing a train's distance from myself

at this window, I can see the woman who was me tugging the gilded blue
spine at the library, shivering to join the meanings of words together. I
  must've thought

the Latin meant *fatal*, not so far from *fate*, two origins
of language folding together like one body hot from a bath, the other

long in the sheets, their limbs quivering to average at the same
temperature, because how is "to love, fatally" so

different than "to be in love with one's fate," the impossibility of a nude
stomach, how a room unseams at first morning light?

Each violin unstitches its voice at my window,
the nightingales turned orchestra, dew
shaking off cypresses as my mug slips in a sheath
of sweat and condensation, coffee dissolving
in cold, and the mirage of a boy arrives

in the throat of a bird: his hands waxing white,
wool-less in the flurry, the care inside his thin
palms as wiggling red segments. If I'd loved
that boy—even if there wasn't just one boy there,
centered in the parabola of kids shaking in their puffed

jackets—if only the chambers of my memory
bear him singularly in the snow in Connecticut, if
I'd loved him better, I would've stepped through
the flakes then, breathed onto his cap, his frosted
lashes, peered through the pink plane of his cheek

to see, too, the living divisions. Young, we dive
our bodies into the wrecks of others' bodies, then
we age to better understand to stand the distance,
how older, calmer, we drive so slowly by car crashes,
swinging our heads, mouthing, "that poor—," how

we squint enrobed in groups before a neighbor's smoking
house, our palms pocketed, our fingernails denting
the seaming, the sirens going and our spongy necks
unable to lock onto spongy neck, my fingerweb unhinged
from your fingerweb: and how to understand the damp

collision of a stranger's body, (yours), floating
delicately in the sheets, the cat's eyes glistening,
and the accident of my blood on your cotton, your ribs
rising up and down, quiet as ghosts? Each time
I enter a memory, it changes with my entrance.

The boy's hands redden and your nakedness washes
like soap, and already I have lost you, your limbs
locked inside the past, and the dying year sweeps
the lessening sun closer to my window, glass straining
in double panes, dark dividing from growing light.

We're Really Not Okay

We're joking about *metzitzah b'peh* and the new wave
of vibrator parties, imagining blue-haired tupperwarers

hand-to-hand with burpless velvety cocks—*and that's how they do
in Denver*, you laugh, the visiting professor who fits in

our bar, in town for a conference. Later, you rub
your fingertips down your blonde corkscrewed hair, and I spill

too much scotch. We've all got our group nicknames: Hollywood and Aztec
God; I'm Caligula, my mouth rabid for the eel

-skinned moon. We bond over benders, divorced,
separated: *our first son died. For ten years my husband couldn't even*

tie his boot. You say, *I didn't want to leave him, squatting on
the foyer joists like that, but*—it's always a never wanting

to leave. I remember
my new lover's daughter assembling

her gingerbread house three days too late
after Christmas, icing glopping each edgy joint,

the foundation dotted to show her
where to put each square in place.

Her father handed her each gumdrop, and out of lack
of emptiness, on dense bread, she swirled on a colored window, sparkling

sugared rose of Notre Dame. One of your curls has slackened.
I tell you, I lost my husband

in Paris. This is only one of the truths, one
lie. In another, he's smoking, his face

all lighter and copper brillo. The beer sweats
clean as a child. Our Aztec God dips in

a finger to Hollywood's martini. If you'd
stick around, I would call you the goddess Demeter. Rumi says,

at a bar or in love, a friend's face reddens,
your cheeks flushed and delicate as English rose.

Golden Shovel: at the Lake's Shore,
I Sit with His Sister, Resting

> *Lost softness softly makes a trap for us.*
> —Gwendolyn Brooks

Michael's skin splinters below the water's line, his navel and all murky and
    lost
like a city from my old life, or that scarf I'd loved, the softness

with which we sink into what disappears, and the country of his groin and
    knees so softly
already blackened. His sister snores below my hands. Her mouth makes

tadpoles. Her breath wet from chemotherapy, I've massaged her a-
sleep. Her shoulders swell their small tides. The air burns leaves.
    I want to want to trap

her sighs, dividing the stillness, in glass, to a Mason jar: breath like smoke
    against a window—: for
this man halved by water. But we sit in sun and grit, watch the waves
    which lose us.

Grave, ma non troppo tratto
For Michael, during the grief of his sister's cancer

> *After great pain, a formal feeling comes—*
> *The Nerves sit ceremonious, like Tombs—*
> *—Emily Dickinson*

This is the hour of touch, your mouth trailing
its small breath song, and a tree soaks morning
where we are calling our dying from the dark,
my tongue sharp-starred with *petite mort*,

unable to say how I feel you as you
enter your own supple death. A woman's
palms unhinge. I screw mine to the creases
opening in your hands, our forms shivering

fevered vein, hardening sun. Why is it
easy through the body to slip free from
the body, but not toward our guarded
hearts? With a word, the sky could drop its net

of constellations. You could phone her, forgive
her your shoulder, the lead, her lost continent,

the small breath song of mourning soaking trees,
the dying dark, and without word, I would
drain the treeline of your freckles, your hips,
into my mouth—your skin tender as water,

thin as the skin of your sister's cheek. You
clasp my hands when we sleep, are showing me
that rest again is possible, and the heater
sounds an ocean through my house, heaving tide

97

of venting in the bedroom; the roses
of your palms. (Your chest blossoms rashes, stamps
against touch.) My darling, you turn quickly
in sentences, number prognoses, then

flicker—your body a lamp, flecked white skein
stretched over your ribs: *muss es sein? Es*

～

muss sein, the dark is dying and without
words, nor hips. Day dissolves to demarcations:
on phones the tiny bells of unvoiced texts,
cloud cleaving a mountain. At Auschwitz,

three girls nap on a bench, the death
wall of Block 11 frenzied with mums,
frills delicate as one skirt's hem. Tourists
stand outside galleries, smoking windows.

(We can only soak in so much before we
tear.) And how does a woman's photoed face blur
into that space beyond fact, called art? You
touch me as if we know what it is to touch.

We drift from our brothers, sisters, the beds
of lost homes beading the horizon—

～

and day dissolves to your demarcations
as I trace my nails your matrices
like sacred texts, score your history. When
I rub the raised shell, scar on your shoulder,

you tell me you think your sister stabbed you
there with a pencil, lead buried your skin
like littleneck clam in sand. If I could
have writ so into another. Though I shot

a rubber band into my brother's eye—:
and lover, *this is the hour of lead,*
remembered, if outlived, our derma
crusting over vessel to account

for what we have lived. (This winter: no belly,
no cry.) And what if it was *you* who'd stabbed

⌒

her? Your nails crescents forging her matrices,
changing her history? Scholars shake in
words, rewriting how we've arrived here, to
what's happened. I've stopped writing for Juárez,

lost the city to birds, and dusk. Men run, clutching
their chests, their guns. Repetition of form
forwards emotion—or does it simply cleave
breath? Space, in chains, I've lied. My brother

was the one who shot me. I cloaked my eye,
no cry. Either way my mother slapped us,
then locked herself behind a wall. We stewed
to hear some sound, to hear her cry: —only

the vent of American air condit
-ioning, *on dit,* "con—," meaning "with," or

⌒

conical: so shared belief shakes history,
our tongues fatty with Latin, French and Greek—
so *conical* memories a sonogram,
my uterus, the watery black cone, tests

and cuttings. Or how once I couldn't wait—
I'd wanted you so bad that morning I soaked
the bed. Your ribs flicker, rise and fall, your
marriage too dripped blood, though your scars are most in

-visible, like mouths unbuttoning in sleep.
Et toutes tes petites morts?, I want to ask,
but know I cannot. This, the hour of touch,
and I can't look you in the eye. Lovers

lock so easily, our arms become bars,
our tongues stilled crows. Grieving, I've loved you less

my deaths, Greek weight of snow, my tongue fatty
with memories, sonograms of my past—
and how have we arrived here, before more
mourning soaks our bed? I cup your ear, its conch

whirling back to shore, your freckles grains of sand,
and the rest of you an ocean, no flag, no
cry. When we kiss, do we suffocate
ourselves our words? Once, at the Pompidou,

before you, I'd lost myself in smoke. Out
the museum, an airy forum: hands
like repeating pendulums, cherry embers
to wintry mouths. We open our lips, cloud

over our mountainous hearts, the pillows
congested with old lovers, and you

whisper a memory: your son soft, the past
clear as sweat. You say he was born ere ruin;
you were afraid to feed him, touch him, strip
him of the wild cleanness of himself. But

our skin dries too quick in the desert, which
maps creeks and valleys into our palms, arroyos
at the centers of our hands. Kiss me, suck
in the words I am dying to say? Speak

this hour now of love, dying, our faces
bright through *effacement*, the thinning cervix...
—*No*, we cobble sex and new cities over
ruins, each temple more silent than

the one echoing below. A phone rings,
stains our quiet light. I trace your stomach

sweat here, clear before ruin, this closeness
trailing ere the hour, thumb your cold mouth.
We left our dead in Juárez. What use are words
now, or the lake I make in your navel, wet

with love? *Grave, allegro, grave,* all
musical movements, orchestras grieving
a falling girl, the night. I divorced a man
when I learned how little I could save. I can't

save you, nor anyone now, these deaths. My heart:
caged starling, and yours flickering under
those ribs. The sun stitches into the drapes,
and soft, now soft, we sink into each other's arms

as freezing persons recollect the snow:
first chill, then stupor, then the letting go.

Safely Watching a Solar Eclipse with Kuya

We hold precision by its tips, geometry of old sun
projecting a pinhole of light so we do not burn

as brother and sister, our bodies revolving, shadows
shifting one to another, shade over shade. An eclipse

can only happen from a fixed point of seeing, and we
see nothing beyond our own shapes, our shoes, this

posterboard bright as a tooth—yet in a few seconds everything
will change: a man will jump into my bed where you have

lain, his black hair grayed as yours sieves white—:
illusions of light, how black, which is nothing, in sun

changes its tone, and how we'll grow to pity each other:
you'll clean cat shit off walls and I'll lose my child, all

the points of us dying as we drift further apart. The sun
isn't a crescent or a loop, it's simply time spreading

and falling, to *here*, *now*, which has never existed, where
you wave your arms as boys do, your brown limbs, feeble

wings. Simple angles, absences of day. New Eclipse, you
shut your eyes tightly as black lines when you imagine

yourself hovering older, rubbing the earth with shadows
from your mechanical shuttle, my astronaut, bloodbird

of my fantasy. I like you better now as I imagine
you: a matrix of mouth and elbow, cicatrix of my memory,

and holding this hole we've cut from the whole, we stand
here waiting, because seeing requires the willing

observer, a superstition, a fixed point of want.

Orison

Dhahran, Saudi Arabia

Horizon: a tinged yolk in measureless dark,
    the city lifting with prayer. At the seam,

        the black earth sharpens its edges. Voices move

bodies up and down, salah of slow
    marionettes, and lips pry open the bright

        teeth, the undulant throat. These are not words

of asking, like *bring her back,* or *Lord, let fall*
    water—rather, a divining

        of intersections: palm to knee, forehead

to soil, man and god, *Allah-hu*—roof tile
    to light. The stomach gurgles, signaling

        hunger. Limbs shrink under white cotton. Day breaks

on a carpet of crowns, the napes below them
    glistening. Later, a man clips an iris,

        readying for death. A woman loses herself

in her daughter's face. The sun hardens, starching
    the sky with her white collar, and the tongue

        retreats, having forgotten its vibrant state.

While My Lover Rests

Night divides from my pillow
as a man and a woman, one taking

breath, and the other, moving
to the pattern of his sleep. The soft

palate clicks as measure, and the dead
drip through the window. Here,

the plates of our women's hips surface
from memory with my nakedness, like a body

and its reflection meeting at the point
of water, and I watch the man alone

in my bed curl, returning. In sleep
we are always aware of the presence

and absence of bodies, and he swims
in delicate ballet to the sheeted

center, knowing the lack of my weight
there. The wind buries herself

against the pane in this lovely, terrible
hour, and all the immigrants I know

of evening are coming to
gather themselves around. Tonight

I am swimming in this
inhalation—exhalation—and the wind,

larger than ever, is wailing, and his
throat relaxes, his uvula aquiver,

and I am listening now and learning
how little my need, in night, to speak.

Touched By Dusk, We Know Better Ourselves

You map my cheeks in gelatinous dark, your torso
floating, a forgotten moon, and a violin

crosses the sheets while you kiss me your mouth
of castanets. I believed once my uncles lived

in trees, from the encyclopedia I'd carried
to my father, *The Philippines*, the Ilongot hunting

from a branch, my father's chin in shadows. I try
to tell you about *distance*, though my body

unstitches, fruit of your shoulder lit by the patio
lamp, grass of you sticky with dew, and all

our unlit places folding, one
into another. By dead night: my face in the pillow,

your knuckles in my hair, my father whipping my
back. How to lift pain from desire, the word

safety from *safe, me*, and the wind
chatters down gutters, rumoring

rain. I graze your stubble, lose my edges mouthing your
name. To love what we can no longer

distinguish, we paddle the other's darkness, whisper
the bed, cry the dying violet hour; you twist

your hands of hard birches, and we peel into
our shadows, the losing of our names.

LINES I'VE STOLEN, AND OTHER NOTES

Epigraphs (p. vii): Photo caption from NASA's *Visible Earth: A Catalog of NASA Images and Animations of Our Home Planet*, titled "El Paso and Ciudad Juárez," October 28, 2014. While in this photo NASA names the border river the US designation, "Rio Grande," in México, the same river is called El Río Bravo del Norte. The second quote is from Ashley Fantz's article "The Mexico Drug War: Bodies for Billions," CNN.com, January 20, 2012.

"If I Die in Juárez" (p. 3): After Stella Pope Duarte's novel of the same title. The US' National Organization for Women estimates the number of femicides that occurred in Juárez to be around four hundred, though some estimate the number to be larger. Most of those killed were maquiladora workers who moved to the city from more rural regions, between seventeen and twenty-two years old (though some victims were one to four years old), and most showed signs of sexual violence. Hundreds more women are still missing. According to Kent Paterson's article "20 Years of Border Femicide" (July 9, 2013, in New Mexico State University's *Frontera NorteSur*), a pattern of disappeared women presented early on (slim, long-haired young women and girls who would vanish, then turn up later, murdered, at sites that served as dumping grounds), and "[m]any of the victims were last reported alive in downtown [Juárez]," characterized in international media as the "maquiladora murders." Unsolved Mexican female homicide is not tied only to Juárez, however. In an article in *Al Jazeera America* (January 4, 2015), Judith Matloff writes, "According to the National Citizen Femicide Observatory, a coalition of 43 groups that document [femicide], six women are [murdered] every day [in México]. Yet only 24 percent of the 3,892 femicides the group identified in 2012 and 2013 were investigated by authorities. And only 1.6 percent led to sentencing."

"13 Ways of Knowing Her" (pp. 4–7): "Mortimer!" and "to keep his anger still in motion" are borrowed from William Shakespeare's play *Henry IV, Part I* when, plotting to drive the king mad, Hotspur contemplates training a starling to repeat the king's prisoner's name, Mortimer. Lines 473–74 read:

"And on my face he turn'd an eye of death / Trembling even at the name of Mortimer." According to Steve Mirsky's article "Antigravity: Call of the Reviled," from a 2008 *Scientific American* article, a group called the American Acclimatization Society, wanting to introduce every bird mentioned in Shakespeare's plays to US sky and soil, released some hundred starlings in Central Park, New York City, between 1890 and 1891. The form sequence steals from Wallace Stevens's "Thirteen Ways of Looking at a Blackbird" and references Susan Wood's "If Grief Were a Bird." The quote from *El Diario*, Ciudad Juárez's main newspaper, is from an article dated May 18, 2014. Finally, on December 31, 2010, thousands of dead birds fell upon Arkansas like black rain.

"My Father's Family Fasts the Slaughter to Feast the Arrival of His Bride" (p. 11): "What did she permit him to see" and "What do we see when we see" are borrowed (the latter slightly changed) from Richard Dove's translation of Joachim Sartorius's poem "Diana." The German originally reads: "Was hat sie ihm erlaubt zu sehen" and "Was sieht man, / wenn man sieht?"

"Meditations on Living in the Desert" (pp. 15–16): After Benjamin Alire Sáenz's poem of the same title.

"Admit Impediments. Love Is Not Love" (p. 17): The title borrows William Shakespeare's second line of Sonnet 116. "Dawn is a damp hand [...] slipped beneath my knee" borrows from Susan Briante's poem "3rd Day of the Rainy Season."

"Continental Split" (p. 18): The act of pressing an elder's hand to one's forehead is a custom of respect in Filipino culture. The younger person first appeals to the elder person, *mano, po*, and the elder then offers his/her hand to bless the bowing person.

"At a Party" (pp. 19–20): In 2009, the flu pandemic of H1N1 hit México, shutting down many cities. Dr. José Ángel Córdova Villalobos, México's secretary of health, states that between March and April, there were over 1,300 reported cases of the virus.

"Panic" (p. 23): In the middle of the drug war between the Sinaloa and Juárez cartels in Ciudad Juárez, México, where the organized crime organizations fought for access to North America primarily through the border cities of Juárez and El Paso, Texas, one group sent gunmen into a drug rehabilitation center on September 2, 2009, killing seventeen patients and wounding two more. During this time, between 2007 and 2011, the city saw a record 3,116 homicides, or an average of eight murders per day, according to the Chihuahua state attorney general's office (though other sources estimate the drug-related deaths to be closer to 10,000 in that same time period). Contrastingly, while the United Nations recognized Juárez as one of the most dangerous cities in the world, its sister city El Paso was ranked as one of the safest cities with a population of more than five hundred thousand, from 2011 to 2013, by CQ Press, which compiled the FBI's Uniform Crime Reports. San Diego was also ranked as one of the United States' safest cities, while cartels raged in Tijuana. Multiple sources agree that more than a hundred thousand murders occurred in México in a six-year period because of the drug war.

"Gedankenexperiments" (pp. 24–25): Perhaps one of the most famous gedankenexperiments is Erwin Schrödinger's, in which he imagines placing a live cat into a sealed steel chamber with radioactive material, tied to a Gieger counter attached to a vial of poison. If a single atom of the radioactive material decays, a relay mechanism will trip the hammer that will break the vial of poison and kill the cat. But because the chamber is sealed, Schrödinger postulates, the observer of the experiment cannot know whether the cat is alive or dead, and according to quantum theory, until the chamber is opened, the cat is both alive and dead, both possibilities still simultaneously true.

"A Loaf of Bread" (p. 26): My ex-husband's close college friend, Robert Castorena, a high school social studies teacher, butchered his wife, Janice Castorena. Before leaving home, he told his young son and daughter to say nothing and not to look behind the master bedroom door. The children lived alone with their dead mother's body for almost two weeks before the boy walked to a local supermarket and shoplifted, hoping the police would catch him. Castorena wrote many letters from his imprisonment, but the one that struck me most was the one in which he wrote that my Christian husband, having re-married (me), was practicing "an abomination to God." The epigraph is quoted from a news article by John Howard from the Associated Press News Archive.

"After Dinner" (p. 27): The phrase "systole, diastole" inverts and borrows Robert Hayden's lyric "diastole, systole" from the poem "Frederick Douglass."

"The Eyes Open to a Cry" (pp. 28–29): The title borrows from the first line of Richard Wilbur's poem "Love Calls Us to the Things of This World."

"In Their Dark Habits" (p. 30): The title steals, slightly, from the ultimate line in Richard Wilbur's poem "Love Calls Us to the Things of This World"; the phrase reads: "And the heaviest nuns walk in a pure floating / Of dark habits, keeping their difficult balance."

"In Step" (pp. 33–35): The poem references Rita Dove's book *American Smooth*.

"Bodies, and Other Natural Disasters" (pp. 46–48): The beginning scene is based on the documentary *A Film Unfinished* (2010), directed by Yael Hersonski, which presents a reel of raw film (labeled "Das Ghetto") shot by Nazi propagandists in Warsaw in May 1942. The reel is composed of Nazi-staged scenes of Jewish life in the ghetto, filmed as perversions of traditional rituals in order to portray an anti-Semitic agenda; for example, ceremonious baths or a circumcision filmed to seem barbaric. Also: Mt. Pinatubo erupted for nine hours near Manila, Philippines, on June 15, 1991, the second largest volcanic eruption of the twentieth century; the tsunami of March 12, 2011, in Miyagi Prefecture, was a result of an earthquake in Japan (measuring 8.9 on the Richter scale). The tsunami, well documented, shows entire towns being washed away. The beautiful Gothic Cathédrale Notre-Dame de Chartres was constructed between 1194 and 1250.

"For Want of Water" (pp. 49–50): On August 2, 2006, the *El Paso Times* reported a case where a thirteen-year-old boy, Julio Hernández, dragged his dead mother's body through the desert after she'd collapsed. The mother, Adela Hernández, had died of dehydration and heat exposure, another story of "illegal" immigration. While in truth a resident called Border Patrol agents to the Santa Teresa Immediate Care Center in Sunland Park, New Mexico, to where the boy had dragged her body behind the building, in the poem I imagine it taking place at Sunland Park Mall in El Paso, Texas, seven miles away.

"Rose is a Rose is a Rose is a Rose" (p. 51): The section title steals Gertrude Stein's famous line from the poem "Sacred Emily."

"At the Symphony: 7 Things I Wish I'd Told You" (pp. 66–67): The line "the jasmine, suffering / / night's guillotine" is stolen from Li-Young Lee's poem "Pillow," whose last two stanzas read: "Everything but sleep. And night begins / / with the first beheading / of the jasmine, its captive fragrance / rid at last of burial clothes."

"Leaving the University Gym" (pp. 72–73): This poem references Marilyn Hacker's poem "Villanelle for D.G.B."

"Tuesday Night in Montparnasse" (pp. 74–75): The epigraph borrows from Dorianne Laux's book and eponymous poem "Facts About the Moon."

"Moment in Storm" (pp. 76–77): Douglas Yates's photo shows a blizzard through a windshield. Yutaka Takanashi's photo is a Cibachrome, part of the Golden Gai Bar series exhibited in 2012 at the Henri Cartier-Bresson Foundation (Paris). The warm, ruddy photos present the Shinjuku Golden Gai district of Tokyo as seemingly recently evacuated ghost spaces, often with shoes stacked in corners or cigarettes askew on ashes. The phrase "responding to the call of this world" steals the ultimate line of Corrinne Clegg Hales's poem "Disappeared: From a Photograph by Gustave LeGray."

"What Is Broken" (p. 89): After Dorianne Laux's poem "What's Broken."

"Before Dawn" (pp. 90–93): The phrase "der schwer gefasste entschluss" is the title of Ludwig van Beethoven's fourth movement in String Quartet No. 16 in F major. The German quoted in the second section are lines stolen from Rainer Maria Rilke's first "Duineser Elegie." Finally, "Young, we dive / our bodies into the wrecks of other's bodies" is stolen from the title of Adrienne Rich's poem "Diving into the Wreck."

"We're Really Not Okay" (pp. 94–95): The term *"metzitzah b'peh"* refers to an ancient Jewish ritual in which the *mohel*, or circumciser, sucks the blood from the penis of a circumcised boy in order to cleanse the circumcision wound.

"Golden Shovel: at the Lake's Shore, I Sit with His Sister, Resting" (p. 96): The epigraph is from Gwendolyn Brooks's poem "The Children of the Poor."

"Grave, ma non troppo tratto" (pp. 97–101): Again from the fourth movement of Beethoven's String Quartet No. 16 in F major, the title comes from the movement's wrestling from *grave* to *allegro*, back and forth, or each theme of "Muss es sein?" with "Es muss sein!" Beethoven introduces this movement with the note "Muss es sein? Es muss sein!" in the music's manuscript, which Milan Kundera later used as a central theme for his character Tomas's sense of will and fate, or his *amor fati*, in the novel *The Unbearable Lightness of Being*. "Space, in chains" steals from Laura Kasischke's book of poems of the same title. The phrases "no belly, no cry" and "no flag, no cry" are stolen from Anne Sexton's poem "The Starry Night," which ends with the last three lines: "from my life with no flag, / no belly, / no cry." And of "effacement, the thinning cervix," the word *effacement*, to be wiped out and erased, is also the medical term for *cervical effacement*, when the cervix thins in childbirth—as in: we are born into effacement as much as mothers bear us in effacement; as Sylvia Plath's speaker in the poem "Morning Song" says: "I'm no more your mother / Than the cloud that distills a mirror to reflect its own slow / Effacement at the wind's hand." Finally, the lines "this is the hour of lead" and the poem's final couplet are stolen from Emily Dickinson's poem "After great pain, a formal feeling comes—" though this poem removes Dickinson's capitalization from those lines.

"Orison" (p. 103): Between the ages of one and five and thirteen and fourteen, I lived with my family in Saudi Arabia. Before I knew how to speak English and later, entering adolescence, I listened to the daily *Salah*, or prayer, projected via loudspeaker over the desert cities of Dhahran and Riyadh. I think of that rhythm of chant as the language of my childhood, where I knew and understood the sounds, though not their meaning.

"Touched By Dusk, We Know Better Ourselves" (p. 105): The title borrows from, and is in conversation with, Mihaela Moscaliuc's poem titled "Everything Touched by Darkness Knows Itself."

CREDITS AND ACKNOWLEDGMENTS

Thank you to the editors of the following journals in which these poems first appeared, sometimes in slightly different form or with another title:

The American Poetry Review: "For Want of Water"

The Bakery: "Kastanyas," "My Father's Family Fasts the Slaughter to Feast the Arrival of His Bride," "School Terrorist Exercise," "Touched By Dusk, We Know Better Ourselves"

Crab Orchard Review: "Bodies, and Other Natural Disasters"

Gulf Coast: "Continental Split," "In Their Dark Habits," "Safely Watching a Solar Eclipse with Kuya"

Huizache: "Meditations on Living in the Desert," "Sea Change"

A Poetry Congeries: "Before Dawn," "Self-Help for Falling (in love) After Divorce," "What Is Broken"

Río Grande Review: "Last Photograph of My Mother Laughing," "Leaving the University Gym"

New England Review: "Orison"

The Normal School: "Grave, ma non troppo tratto," "Old Beds and Hollywood," "Tuesday Night in Montparnasse," "You Say You Can't Sleep"

Winning War Writers: "After Dinner in El Paso," "The Eyes Open to a Cry," "Panic"

"Moment in Storm" first appeared in the anthology *Open to Interpretation: Intimate Landscapes*, and "Golden Shovel: at the Lake's Shore I Sit with His Sister, Resting" appeared in the *Golden Shovel Anthology* on the work of Gwendolyn Brooks (University of Arkansas Press, 2017).

Profound gratitude to, first and foremost, judge Gregory Pardlo (to whom I owe my path in poetry from this point on); Daniel Halpern and Beth Dial of the National Poetry Series, who do such important work for us all; and Helene Atwan, Beth Collins, Nicholas DiSabatino, Maya Fernandez, Tom

Hallock, Alyssa Hassan, Susan Lumenello, Melissa Nasson, Louis Roe, and the incredible people of Beacon Press, without whom this would not be a book. Thank you to my brilliant family in Michael Topp, Adam Topp, and Esme Topp. For your support and guidance, thanks to Albert Abonado; Neil Aitken; Rosa Alcalá; Linnea Alexander; Chuck Ambler; Gloria Ambler; Maram Al-Masri; Rick Barot; James Bertolino; Tara Betts; Arlene Biala; Natalie Bourdon; Carol Brochin; Sharon Bryan; Ezra Cappell; Cyrus Cassells; Steven Church; Andrea Cote; John Crawford; Maceo Dailey; Howard Daudistel; Marcia Hatfield Daudistel; Justin Desmangles; Lucía Durá; José de Piérola; Ruben Espinosa; Joshua Fan; Christine Foerster; Sesshu Foster; Sarah Gambito; Mimi Riesel Gladstein; Eugene Gloria; Juan Guzmán; Corrinne Clegg Hales; Juan Felipe Herrera; Lee Herrick; Jack Hirschman; Luisa Igloria; Janine Joseph; Joseph Legaspi; Franny Levine; my poetry hero, Philip Levine; Diana Natalicio; Eric Parker; Emma Pérez; Norbert Portillo; Bino Realuyo; Ishmael Reed; Paisley Rekdal; Barbara Jane Reyes; Benjamin Alire Sáenz; Elizabeth Scanlon; Liz Scheid; Tim Skeen; Leon Stokesbury; Eileen Tabios; Cheryl Torsney; Jon Tribble; Lex Williford; Patricia Witherspoon; and Andre Yang. Thank you to the University of Texas at El Paso, particularly my students Aldo Amparan, Abigail Carl-Klaasen, James Cherry, Betty Fisher, Lupe Méndez, Michael McBirnie, Alessandra Narvaez, Aaron Romano-Meade, and Natalie Scenters-Zapico, and to each graduate and undergraduate writer, from whom I have learned more of poetry than they from me.

Jorge Salgado

Born in Manila and raised in the United States and Saudi Arabia, SASHA PIMENTEL is also the author of *Insides She Swallowed*, winner of the 2011 American Book Award. Selected by Philip Levine, Mark Strand, and Charles Wright as a finalist for the 2015 Rome Prize in Literature (American Academy of Arts and Letters), Pimentel's work has been published in such journals as *American Poetry Review*, *New England Review*, and *Crazyhorse*. She teaches poetry as a professor in the bilingual MFA Program in Creative Writing at the University of Texas at El Paso, on the border of Ciudad Juárez, México.

GREGORY PARDLO's collection *Digest* (Four Way Books) won the 2015 Pulitzer Prize for Poetry. His other honors include fellowships from the Guggenheim Foundation, the National Endowment for the Arts, and the New York Foundation for the Arts; his first collection, *Totem,* won the APR/ Honickman Prize in 2007. He is also the author of *Air Traffic*, a memoir in essays, forthcoming from Knopf.